NOV 7 '67 SHAFTER		
APR 1 6 '75 TEHACHAPI		
SEP 1 6 '76 MOJAVE		
JAN 5 '81 OILDALE		

A Snail's A Failure Socially

Illustrated by Kit Dalton

A Snail's A Failure Socially

Socially

And Other Poems, Mostly About People

KAYE STARBIRD

J.B. Lippincott Company

Philadelphia and New York

For Gladys and Francis
With Love

Contents

A Snail's A Failure Socially

The Fishing Lady

I've met a Miss or Mrs. Hanks
Who fishes near the alder banks,
Rowing in summer, fall, and spring
Along the creek where blackbirds sing.

I have a hidden place I go
Where I can sit and watch her row
Back and forth on the creek below.
Not fat or thin or young or old,
She fishes if it's hot or cold,
Always dressed in a hat that's red,
Some trousers and a denim blouse,
While thoughts keep running through my head
Like: has she friends? . . . and where's her house?

I wouldn't know her name, except
One evening when her boat was tied
I went to where the boat was kept
And pushed the alder boughs aside
And saw upon the rowboat planks
A notice: PROPERTY OF HANKS.

And then I dug some worms one day,
Hoping there might be more to learn,
And took them in a thoughtful way
Down to the beach around the turn.
But when I waved the earthworm tin
And shouted could she use some worms,
Although she rowed her rowboat in,
We never got on talking terms.

She put the worms upon a shelf
And covered them and told me thanks;
And when I introduced myself,
She murmured: well, *her* name was Hanks
And handed me some perch . . . and then
She rowed her rowboat out again.

So while I wish I knew for sure,
Up in my secret thinking spot,
Whether the lady's rich or poor
And if she's happy or she's not
And if she's Mrs. Hanks or Miss . . .
I still don't know. I just know this:
She fishes near the alder banks
And answers to the name of Hanks.

The Signs

Today I listened to a crow that cawed
Somewhere out in the windy maple wood
And watched a darkened brook the sun had thawed
Swirling around a rock on which I stood.

Although the hills and hollows still held snow,
And skies, no longer angry, still pretended,
My private calendar—a brook and crow—
Told me another wintertime had ended.

Benny McBlore

Benny McBlore, who's fifty or more,
Has rather a low I.Q.,
Which means he can't do all of the jobs
That fifty-year-olds should do.
His mind stopped growing when he was young,
But—unperturbed by its slowing—
Benny McBlore looked out of his door
And noticed what else was growing.

Each spring in Maine when the ferns unfurled
And Benny was sure the snows were through,
He'd gaze in awe at the wondrous world
Where trees and bushes and blossoms grew . . .
And stick a bud in his visored hat
And rake and harrow and hoe the ground,
Wishing the world would stay like that
With everything growing all year round.

And late one summer his wish came true.
As he was weeding his dwindling garden,
Some kindly Summer People he knew
Who happened to see him, begged his pardon
And said they needed a man like Benny
For winter work at their place down south.
A man like Benny?
There weren't too many.
A smile crept slowly up Benny's mouth;

And Benny answered: "I read and spell,
And also, I drive a car right well,

And seeing I like to watch things grow,
I reckon I'll get some wheels and go."

So, buying an ancient, seatless bus
And sticking a dahlia in his cap,
Benny McBlore, with miles to explore,
Got some supplies and a seaboard map
And giving his horn a farewell toot,
He went down south by the coastal route,
Where now he lives for half of the year
(The chilly half, when northerners fuss),
Then heads for Maine when the spring is here,
Happy and proud in his yellow bus.

The yellow bus is a home to Benny,
A special home with special décor,
Equipped with lockers
And Boston rockers,
Besides a bed and rug on the floor;
And vases and urns
Of flowers and ferns
And paper packets of moss and vines
And cartons of roots
And bamboo shoots
And bags of pine cones from Georgia pines,
And boxes of food and dishes, *plus*
The decorations outside his bus:
For instance, posters of Indian maids

And bumper signs from the Everglades
And glow-in-the-dark Miami stickers
And Kewpie dolls
In knickers
And slickers,
And printed pleas like DON'T OVERLOAD
And DRIVE WITH CAUTION and SHARE THE
    ROAD,
Along with items that bob and sail
Like rabbits' feet and a fox's tail.

And up in Maine where natives lose track
Of whether the winter's had its fling,
They see when Benny McBlore gets back
And say, "There's Benny. It must be spring."
And Benny McBlore, with treasures galore,
Delightedly gives his knee a slap,
And hollering "Hi"
As friends go by
He sticks a pansy into his cap
And thinks of the wondrous world he's found
Where things keep growing the whole year round.

The Problem

This morning Doctor Heath
(The dentist) drilled my teeth
And filled them with some silver sitting handy,
And looking pretty mad
Because my teeth were bad,
He ordered me to stay away from candy.

Then later I went by
To visit Doctor Bly,
Who gave me shots for polio and flu;
And since he can't recall
That I'm no longer small,
He offered me a lollypop or two.

I wondered what reply
To give to Doctor Bly.
Was I to say that candy ruins teeth?
Or let the matter drop
And *eat* a lollypop
And risk the future wrath of Doctor Heath?

The Trout

Hundreds of fish
Both large and small
Were trying to climb
The waterfall.
There with the water
Booming and crashing,
I watched them leaping;
I watched them splashing,
Struggling up over stony shelves,
Then slipping back
In spite of themselves.

Off near the bankside
Lone and bereft,
Trapped in a pool
The snows had left,
A weary trout
Swam slowly about,
Moving through water warm to the touch,
Feeling a fool
And circling the pool
Apparently not expecting much.

So out of kindness
(Not out of love)
I caught the trout in a gentle fist
And flung it into the stream above,

The upper stream
The other fish missed.

And while I stood
In the bankside laurel
I couldn't think
Of a proper moral;
And yet as I watched
No fish at all
Ever got past
The waterfall.
Some of them feared it.
Some overplayed it,
And only the trapped trout
Finally made it.

Angleworms

Down in the darkness under the ground
The silent angleworms slink around.

From day to day and from week to week
They pass each other and never speak.
And yet, if angleworms talked like us,
What would they really care to discuss?

Meeting together there in the murk,
What would they mention? Their dreams? Their work?
Or how some neighbor down by the drain
Got washed away in a recent rain?

The hopes of an angleworm are rare.
It's true that a worm can turn . . . but where?

What thinking worm would hasten to swap
His underworld life for life Up Top,
Carelessly quitting his earthside hush
To take up residence in a thrush?

With not much news and none of it good,
What would angleworms say if they could?
Would any of them discuss their looks?
Or fishing season? Or fishing hooks?

I guess a worm, not being a fretter,
Just figures the less that's said the better.

Miss Tabor

Our middle-aged neighbor
Whose name is Miss Tabor
Has never been anyone's wife.
She has no relations
Who come on vacations
(With children and puppies and such irritations)
To mess up her house and her life.

Miss Tabor is little and jumpy and thin
And doesn't like joking or joshing.
Her home, though it's ugly, is neat as a pin
And wet from continual washing.
Her kitchen on most of the mornings I stop
Has wall-to-wall puddles, which mean
That somewhere Miss Tabor, with rags or a mop,
Is seeking new vistas to clean.

So going around to the front of the house
I walk to the den or the halls
Where—hard at her labor—
I find that Miss Tabor
Is swabbing some woodwork or walls.
And if, as we chatter,
I duck through her ladder
And head for a sofa nearby,
I carefully hover
Until I discover
If all of the cushions are dry.

Since cleaning is taxing
Miss Tabor—relaxing—
Sits down now and then and crochets,
Perhaps on a coaster
Or lid for her toaster
Or bags for her dresser sachets.
And after crocheting
It goes without saying
(With carpets shampooed till they're frayed
And ceilings cleansed amply
And shelves glowing damply)
She washes the things she's crocheted.

Thus, rinsing and rubbing
And scouring and scrubbing,
She neatens her household with pride,
So full of endeavor
She's blind to whatever
Goes on in the village outside.
Though Aprils keep coming
With woodpeckers drumming
And barn swallows dipping and zooming,
She feels it's more urgent
To wield a detergent
Than look at the bridal wreath blooming.

A Snail's a Failure Socially

A snail's a failure socially,
Which means you very seldom see
A crowd of happy, laughing snails
Collected all at once.
The reason's this: when asked to dine
A snail could answer "Yes" or "Fine,"
But if he lived a field away
The trip would take him months.

In short, the most excited snail,
Though pleased to hit the party trail,
Could promptly tidy up and take
A shortcut through the clover;
But asked to Easter luncheon—say—
And getting there Columbus Day,
There'd be at least an even chance
He'd find the party over.

Whistling Willie

Remember Whistling Willie's market
Over on Center Street,
The dingy store with the sticking door
Where everyone went for meat?
All of a sudden they tore it down
And put up a Super Shop,
A giant market with miles of aisles
And neon lights at the top.

And something nobody seems to know
Is: where did Whistling Willie go?

Whistling Willie was small and round
With hair like a dried-out thistle,
And fixing sausage or hamburg-ground
Or weighing chicken-legs by the pound
Or getting a pot roast cut and bound,
He'd whistle.

Willie's answers were always brief
When customers tried to chat.
He'd just say "Yup" as he rolled some beef
Or trimmed some tenderloin fat.
Or else he'd finish the interview
By flexing his aching wrists,
And standing there with his hair askew
Among the flypaper twists . . .
He'd frown a little before he spoke
To show that his thoughts were weighty,
Then mutter, giving the meat a poke,
"I make it a dollar-eighty."

Willie was mild and quiet, too,
But now and again he bristled,
Like once I asked him whether he knew
The words to a song he whistled,
And Willie said to me: "Moons and Junes!
So maybe a singer reads them,
But me, I'm just a whistler of tunes,
And all of them words. Who needs them?"

The Super Shop has meat in a case.
You wheel up a cart and park it.
And I suppose, if you like the place,
It's better than Willie's market.
The workers smile in the Super Shop
And carry your grocery sack
And say they're glad you happened to stop
And urge you to hurry back.

The thing I keep on wondering, though,
Is: where did Whistling Willie go?

Rain

When birds chirp slowly
And bees stop humming,
I'm pretty certain
A rainstorm's coming.
Without knowing why
I pace about
And notice the leaves
Turn inside out,
While down by the pond
A peeper cries,
And somewhere another one
Replies.

Then quick as a flash
A rush of rain
Hoses the house
And darkens the lane
And pounds the roof
And puddles the lawn,
Till just as quickly
The rain is gone,
Leaving behind it
Dripping for hours
The lilac bush
With its foam of flowers.

The Sisters

The Widow Rose and Widow Fay
Are sister widow-ladies.
They're seventy if they're a day
Or maybe in their eighties.
The Widow Fay, who's short and square,
Wears mostly tweedy clothes
And braids and pins her iron hair,
But not the Widow Rose.

The Widow Rose wears frills and bows
And poufs her hair in clouds
And never goes to town to shop
Because she hates the crowds.
So while she fixes scones for tea
The Widow Fay, who copes,
Goes stalking through the A & P
And punching cantaloupes.

In summer when the Widow Fay
Gardens and tends the yard,
The Widow Rose with "ah's" and "oh's"
Says not to work too hard;
And as she coolly strolls around
Picking bouquets and pleading,

The Widow Fay in disarray
Keeps clipping things and weeding.

The Widow Rose deplores the way
They can't find help to hire
And in her orchid negligee
In winter by the fire
She tries to make the house look gay
And fans the flames a-glow
And waits until the Widow Fay
Comes in from sweeping snow . . .

Then putting teacups on a tray
And treating them like playthings,
She gossips while the Widow Fay
Seems disinclined to say things.
But when they each have had a scone,
Safe from the wintry weather,
They're glad that since they live alone
They live alone together.

Cockroaches

A leaf bug comes from an egg in June
Before it can live and thrive.
A green moth comes from a curled cocoon,
A honeybee from a hive.
But though in all of the insect books
Such varied sources make sense,
Like water beetles coming from brooks
Or caterpillars from tents . . .
The thing that really puzzles me some
In the way of bug affairs
Is: why do cockroaches always come
From The People Living Upstairs?

Tony

Tony's drying dishes
And cleaning out the hall,
And all he did was use the phone
To make a friendly call.

For Tony's being punished
(Which happens more and more)
Because he's only four years old
And much too smart for four.
A case of what I mean is this:
His parents thought it prattle
When Tony asked if he could phone
His uncle in Seattle.
So Tony's parents answered "Sure,"
Only to check too late
And find he'd talked from coast to coast
For fifty minutes straight,
Which started Tony hollering
He wasn't fresh or bad,
He'd asked to call Seattle,
And they'd let him, and he had.

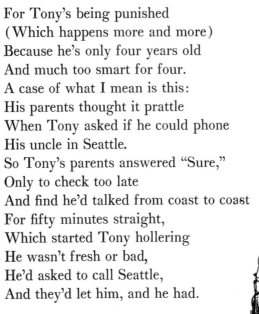

Tony's in the corner
Upon the Naughty Stool,
And all because he tried to do
The work in nursery school.

When Tony tired of coloring,
To vary his routine
Miss Keith, his teacher, had him make
A bowl of plasticene.

But even though he made the bowl
Miss Keith looked fierce and smitten
To note that on the back of it
MADE IN JAPAN was written.
And since it didn't seem to help
When Tony told Miss Keith
He only wrote what all cheap bowls
Had written underneath . . .
Not really liking fierceness much,
He took a pencil WHOOM
And fired it in a rubber band
Across the silent room.

Tony's in the corner
Where he's been sent again
Because—at four—he reads and writes
Like someone nine or ten.

Upset about the Bowl Affair,
Miss Keith—appearing grimmer—
Decided Tony might enjoy
A lovely first-grade primer.
The trouble was that later on
When she was less forbidding
And asked if Tony liked the book,
He answered: "Are you kidding?
'My dog can run. My ball is fun.
My kitten is a pet.
See Mother cook. See Baby look.'

How boring can you get?"
And just to warn some future child
The story wasn't bearable,
He scribbled on the title page:
"Don't read this book. It's terrible."

Since Tony, what with this and that,
Was no example-setter,
The teacher said to stay at home
Until he acted better;
Which didn't bother Tony much,
For what could be forlorner
Than spending half your waking hours
Restricted to a corner?

So now he's sweeping sidewalks
And beating scatter rugs,
And though he keeps his mind alert
By watching birds and bugs.

He's sick of being punished
(Which happens more and more)
Because he's only four years old
And much too smart for four.
He's sick of how his mother says
In accents sad and moan-y:
"He's brilliant, *but*
I don't know what
We'll ever *do* with Tony."

A Moose Is Loose

There's a moose
That's loose,
The radio says,
So people had best watch out.
You can't make a truce
If the moose
That's loose
Has something he's miffed about.
Besides, the moose may easily have
A mate that he introduces,
And if you're afraid of *one* miffed moose,
Just think about *two* miffed mooses.
And that isn't all. It stands to reason
Because each separate moose
Has veins that throb in the May Day season
With vigor and jungle juice,
A couple of animals like that
Aren't halted by traps or nooses,
Especially when they're all revved up
With vigor and jungle juices.

What's more, if both of the beasts produce
Some friends and maybe a niece
(Not both *together*, I didn't mean.
The thing I meant was *apiece*)
With moose after moose
Out running loose,
Don't look for problems to cease.
The antlered army could cook your goose
And all of the neighbors' geese.

The Gliddens

We know some people named Glidden,
A couple without much charm,
Who live in a big and gloomy house
And view the world with alarm.
Yearlong they sit in their parlor
Where nothing is going on
And grimly talk about Sad Events
With most of their curtains drawn.

Whenever I go there calling
Believing I'll make them glad,
I find I never can cheer them up.
They're happier being sad.
I say it's a lovely morning,
And Mister Glidden says "Oh?"
An hour ago when he stepped outside
He figured it looked like snow.

I say would they like a kitten,
A tiger kitten, a male?
And Mrs. Glidden says Heavens, No!
She's never known it to fail . . .
You start with a nice boy-kitten
To catch the mice and the rats,

Then find it's a *girl*, and pretty soon
You're up to your neck in cats.

One day I was horseback riding
And showed them the horse I'd ridden,
And Mister Glidden looked sorrowful
And—nodding to Mrs. Glidden—
He warned me horses were tricky
And probably I'd get spilled.
A friend of theirs had a horse, he said,
And rode it and *she* got killed.

I take the Gliddens some roses;
They ask about rose-bush bugs.
I say it's nice that the sun is out;
They tell me it fades the rugs.
I pick them a box of apples;
They wonder if worms are hidden.
In short, since all that I say or do
Seems either wrong or forbidden . . .
I've finally come to realize
You just can't gladden a Glidden.

Idaho

Farmers out in Idaho
Plant potatoes, row on row.
Then before the green vines show
Every farmer has to go
Daily hoe-ing with his hoe
Up and down the rows till—lo—
Finally potatoes grow.

This, potato farmers know:
What comes up must start below;
What you reap you have to sow;
What you grow you have to hoe.

If you don't like farming, though,
    And you've never *tried* a hoe
    Or you hate to guide a hoe
    Or you can't abide a hoe,
    Stay away from Idaho.

The Montreal Track

There's Queen Anne's lace in the railroad track.
It sways and whispers above the ties,
Where once the trains went clickety-clack
From Boston to Montreal and back,
Their whistles echoing down the skies.

My father says that when he was small
Each day the train came by like a friend;
And out on the fence-bars, feeling tall,
He'd sit and muse about Montreal,
Watching the engine circle the bend.

Or else at dusk he'd run to the bars
Whenever he heard the whistle wail;
And suddenly, puffing steam and stars,
The train would come with its snake of cars,
Carrying passengers, freight and mail.

And he could see through the headlamp's flush
The engineer as he waved his hand,
And later see, in the noise and rush,
The people inside on seats of plush
Blurring a little but looking grand.

And watching the passing people there,
My father would chew a piece of bark
And think how future children would stare

When *he* was grown and going somewhere,
Riding in style through the dropping dark.

Of course, my father couldn't have known
When he was maybe a boy of ten
And sat imagining all alone
The journeys he'd take when he was grown . . .
The silver track would be silent then.

And though at night when the wind is high
My father tells me he's apt to dream
That out where the meadow meets the sky
Again the trains go clacketing by,
Wailing their whistles and shooting steam . . .

Next day when he hears the robins call
And looks from his window off through space,
The track is empty to Montreal,
And nothing moves there, nothing at all,
Except the wind in the Queen Anne's lace.

Three Nuns

Once in the park
When I rode my bike,
I met three nuns
Who were just alike.
They all wore gowns
Of fluttery black
That hid their shapes
In front and in back,
With beads (in front)
For saying their graces
And starched white haloes
Around their faces.

They all had glasses
To ease their eyes.
And all three nuns
Were a nunlike size.
And when they saw me
They smiled as one
And said together:
"Good day, my son,"
Then moved on by
In a kind of glide,
Nodding in unison
Side by side.

Mrs. Riley

Mrs. Riley has a beau again.
She's brought him over here to visit twice.
He's not like Mrs. Riley's other men,
But, even so, my parents say he's nice.
His name is Horace Hopper and he's small,
With glasses that keep sliding down his nose;
But Mrs. Riley's brought him twice to call,
A thing she very seldom does with beaux.

Mrs. Riley's life keeps rearranging.
She's lost a lot of husbands, namely three.
And, while it seems her luck could stand some changing,
The time I said as much she looked at me . . .
Then, staring at a dying fireplace ember
As if she stared at something in the past,
She said her luck was good enough, remember.
The only trouble was it didn't last.

Mrs. Riley may be forty-five
Or may be older. Still, you get the feeling
That though she isn't witty, she's alive,
And though she isn't pretty, she's appealing.
She never laughs too loud or talks too much.
She's not possessive and she isn't wily;
So men, pursued by giddy girls and such,
Would somehow rather be with Mrs. Riley.

Mrs. Riley's men (don't ask me *which* ones)
Buy her bouquets . . . and perfume by the ounce;
But while she's had some handsome beaux and rich ones,
It's what a person *is*, she says, that counts.
It's not a case of who's the highest bidder,
Since marriage isn't *things*, she says, but years,
And nothing that a lady should consider
Unless the proper gentleman appears.

She doesn't mention who she means is proper,
But when she brings somebody twice to call,
It's possible she *may* mean Horace Hopper,
For though he's bald and isn't very tall . . .
They go for evening walks around the bay now,
And both of them appear so proud and smiley
It looks to me like almost any day now
More wedding bells will ring for Mrs. Riley.

Elephants

An elephant on a TV set
Is pretty much like a household pet,
Exotic, perhaps, but harmless.
He's usually pictured hauling things,
For instance, arrogant Eastern kings,
A chore that he must find charmless . . .
Though that's a thought that the kings avoid
Until some elephant gets annoyed
And leaves them crumpled or armless.

Meanwhile, an elephant seems so glamorous
Tourists to Africa carry cameras,
Hoping to get a shot of one;
Then saying "Tisk" when they all mean "Tusk"
They madly flee through the tropic dusk,
Alarmed at the bulk and trot of one,
Deciding that since there seems to be
A lot of an elephant to see,
It's silly to see a lot of one.

The Walk

I had no destination in mind,
No clue to what I was nearing.
I merely walked up a wooded hill
And walked and walked through the woods until
I came to a halfway-clearing.

Since every forest opens and closes
I shrugged and started to pass,
When suddenly I saw yellow roses
Bright in the hip-high grass;
And giving the flowers a second glance
I knew as I thought things through
That yellow roses don't grow by chance.
Only the pink ones do.

So while a chipmunk watched from a tree
I wandered out in the open space.
There wasn't anything much to see
Except a silent, meadowy place.
But just about then I stubbed my toe
On what I guessed was a hidden rock
And gazing into the grass below
I caught the glint of a shattered clock,
Which made me search a bit to the right

Where I discovered a cracked blue bowl
And—under some timber out of sight—
The stones of a cellar hole.

The chipmunk made a chittery sound
As I stooped over among the weeds
And pushed the timber away and found
A metal comb and some coral beads
And runners off of a children's sled
And part of an old brass bed.

Before I knew it, I reached and put
The coral beads on a cellar stone
And—tapping the bedstead with my foot—
I missed some people I'd never known.
And while I thought of their lives . . . and how
They once were there, but they weren't there now,
The chipmunk ran away from his tree,
And no one was left but me.

A cloud passed over the high-up sky,
And what I wanted to do was cry,
But what I finally did was stand
And comb my bangs with the metal comb
And catch a butterfly in my hand
And let it loose, going home.

The Toadstool Town

Over in the singing cedars
Summers, when the plants were showing,
Back when I was six or seven
I would notice toadstools growing:
Yellowish and grayish toadstools,
Orange ones and sometimes brown,
Looking like the roofs of houses,
Looking like a tiny town.

Then the years began to hurry.
Seasons flew away on wings.
I became involved in schoolwork,
Reading books and learning things.
Changing and becoming older,
Busy with the friends I met,
I forgot the toadstool village;
Yet I didn't quite forget.

Finishing with school last summer,
One day, feeling ill at ease,
I discovered I was walking
Over toward the cedar trees.
Getting in among the cedars,
Sheltered from the wind and sun,
When I looked around for toadstools,
None of them were there. Not one.

Though I knew the years kept moving,
Though I knew the seasons passed,
Something that I loved had ended,
Something that I thought would last.

I was pretty old for fancies,
Fancies of the childhood kind.
Anybody going forward
Has to leave the past behind.
Still, I spent a lot of mornings
Walking up the slopes and down,
Wandering among the cedars,
Searching for the toadstool town.

The New Life

Mrs. Otis has sold her house
Which makes her various friends assume
That since she has an apartment now
She must be crowded in just one room;
But when I asked how it seemed without
Her ancient, rambling country estate,
She gazed around at her rented home
And answered frankly, it seemed just great.
No roofs to mend,
No gardens to weed,
No cats or puppies or fish to feed.
"Why, I can leave on a minute's notice.
A lovely feeling," said Mrs. Otis.

So then I said (since I knew she planned
A trip abroad the following day)
I'd gladly do any household chores
She wanted done while she was away.
And Mrs. Otis replied, "How nice!
I rather hope, if you get a chance,
You'll feed the bird in my cuckoo clock
And water my plastic pansy plants."

The Almost-Hermit

Down by the shining sea there's a house of stone
And in it a quiet man who lives alone.
All year the ocean thunders onto his shore,
And over his roof the white clouds blow like kites;
But what on earth does he live alone there for?
How does he spend the endless days and nights?

He's not too old a hermit as hermits go.
His hair is cut, and his clothes are fairly new.
The time I happened over and said hello
I found he spoke politely when spoken to.
But after a little while I felt un-needed,
And then there came a kind of a talking lull,
And I fell silent suddenly, just as he did,
And saw that he was watching a wheeling gull.

The furniture in his house is rather mixed
With books and empty coffee cups everywhere.
The day I called, a rabbit whose foot he'd fixed
Was lying on the arm of an easy chair.
He had a couple of pictures, maybe good ones,
Like one of hills and one of a church's steeple.
He had some sculptures, too, some marble and wood ones,
But all of birds and animals. None of people.

I bravely asked, as the clouds outside were blowing,
Why he lived by himself . . . and with eyelids shut
He answered something started and just kept going.
But that was all. He stopped and never said what.
Instead, he opened his eyes and looking stern
He put the coffee back on the stove to brew it.
I hoped when I left he'd say to please return,
But though I paused on the porch he didn't do it.

Down by the shining sea there's a house of stone
And in it a quiet man who lives alone.
All year the ocean thunders onto his shore,
And over his roof the white clouds blow like kites;
But what on earth does he live alone there for?
How does he spend the endless days and nights?

The Bumble Bee

A last, slow-moving bumble bee
Spins in a crumpled aster,
While winds, so calm and quiet once,
Whirl faster now and faster.

I wonder if the bee is sad
Because his friends are gone
And mourns to see the rose-bush leaves
Blowing about the lawn . . .

Or whether, like an old, old man,
He just accepts what is,
Glorying, as he ends his days,
In one more day that's his.

The Statue

Pruitt Palmer who fought with a gun
To help the Revolution get won
After the war remarked to a friend:
"Now that the fighting's come to an end,
I think the country could use some knowledge.
Tomorrow I'd better start a college."

Whereupon, flinging his gun aside,
He founded Palmer College and died.
And yet whenever I climb the hill
In order to view the college scene,
I get the feeling he's living still
For—straight and tall on the chapel green—
With granite hair pulled back in a queue
And granite breeches and jacket, too,
A statue of Pruitt Palmer stands
Holding a book in a soldier's hands
And grinding a booted heel upon
The broken butt of a granite gun.

Year after year the students pass
Below the statue going to class,
While ignorant pigeons stop to rest
High on the granite arms or chest,
And every autumn
The leaves of red
Cling like a crown to the statue's head,
And later the snows
Drift over its clothes
And give it a cape of white instead.

And each Commencement, when students file
Up on the chapel steps and down,
In typical graduation style
The statue wears a cap and a gown.
And peering off through the flowering trees
And college buildings that stretch for miles,
In robes that rustle around its knees,
It almost looks like the statue smiles.

There by the chapel, tall and commanding,
Holding a book in his soldier's hands,
It seems that Pruitt Palmer is standing
Where really only his statue stands.
It even seems that he hears the talk
Of people walking the campus walk
And smells the flowers
And watches the towers
Where ivy gleams in the summer sun
And under his heel
Can almost feel
The broken butt of the granite gun.

The Leaf Pile

I raked the leaves today, and after a while
I piled them near the steps in a jumping pile;
And later on, with supper and homework ended,
As Mother sat in the dining room and mended,
I said: "The moon is shining under the eaves.
Tonight's a perfect night for jumping in leaves.
Too bad you're old and busy with socks and sleeves."

My mother squinted down at a stocking heel
And answered, "Age isn't age. It's how you feel;
And now I'm feeling sick of this mending box.
Tonight's no night for working on sleeves and socks."
And, raising the blind to get the moon in sight,
She seemed to ponder a bit and said, "You're right.
It *is* a perfect jump-in-the-leaf-pile night."

And then she closed her box so loudly it thumped,
And both of us went out on the steps and jumped.

The Gypsy Woman

Carnival-times, there's a gypsy woman
Who comes whenever the sideshow comes,
Wearing some beads and a mask of makeup
And clothes the color of ripened plums,
And also wearing, with scores of bracelets,
Rings on her fingers . . . even her thumbs.

Some people think the woman's a phony.
Others believe she's gaudy and bold,
Sitting all day in her tent of orange
Under a sign saying FORTUNES TOLD,
Calling to anyone, "Hi there, dearie,"
And coyly flashing her teeth of gold.

Teenager girls when they see the gypsy
Goggle or giggle, with arms a-link.

Teenager boys, being somewhat shyer,
Shuffle their feet as they nudge and wink,
While nervous lovers pause as they're passing,
Asking each other, "What do you think?"

For years I wondered about my future,
All that was coming and hadn't been,
So last year seeing the gypsy woman
Sitting and rubbing her powdered chin,
I found a dollar and smiled politely
And dodged the tent-flap and went on in.

At first she told me I'd meet a stranger
And probably take a journey soon,
And then she murmured, "Forget it, dearie,"

Continuing in a slurry croon,
"The moon looks down on a million rivers.
The rivers look at only one moon.

"No, that isn't right," she added, sipping
A glass of wine and heaving a sigh.
"The sky looks down on a million mountains.
The mountains look at only one sky.
Dearie," she said to me, "time's your fortune.
Whatever happens, don't wish time by."

And suddenly she looked old and friendless,
And, not understanding what she meant,
I told myself that she *was* a phony
And dropped my dollar and turned and went,
And yet I think I'll always remember
The words the gypsy said in the tent.

Who'll be the sky, and who'll be a mountain?
The moon or a river? No one knows,
Except, perhaps, for the gypsy woman
Whose fortune is over, I suppose;
And so she just keeps making a living,
Going wherever the sideshow goes.

She isn't young, and she won't get younger.
She's learned with fortunes you take what comes,
And if you happen to be a gypsy
You dress in clothes the color of plums,
Garishly wearing
Without much caring
Rings on your fingers . . . even your thumbs.

The Sleet Storm

Last night we had a heavy rain
That later on began to freeze;
And when I woke today the ice
Had covered roofs and roads and trees.

The bushes and the lawns were glass,
The lamp-posts and the hedges, too.
The hedge-twigs snapped like capgun shots
When I reached down and broke a few.

Sucking an ice thermometer
I climbed upon the front-porch rail
And watched the city glittering
Like something in a fairy tale;
And thinking how the crystal world
Would melt into the same drab town,
I swung my arm along the eaves
And xylophoned the icicles down.

The Palace

High above the river,
High above the sands,
Halfway up the mountain
Patrick's palace stands.
Past the glassless windows
Birds fly to and fro,
Through the rooms abandoned there
Sixty years ago.

Handsome Patrick Randall
All for Alice Tate
Brought the house from England
Wood and stone and slate.
All for lovely Alice
Soon to be his bride,
Patrick built the house again
On the mountainside.

Patrick Randall, wanting
Only lovely Alice,
Thought she needed settings,
Thought she wished a palace.
Alice, thinking settings
New and strange to handle,
Only acted pleased to please
Handsome Patrick Randall.

While the workmen labored
Finishing the palace,
One day on a balcony

Laughing, lovely Alice . . .
Plunging through a railing
High and incomplete,
Wanting only Patrick's arms,
Died at Patrick's feet.

Wild with love and sorrow,
Furious at fate,
Patrick hurtled weeping
Through the gateless gate.
Crying, "Take my palace,"
Sobbing, "I'm no prince,"
Patrick Randall went away.
No one's seen him since.

On the summer morning
Lovely Alice died,
Carpenters and masons
Laid their tools aside.
Gardeners who carried
Bushes yon and thither,
Left the naked roots to wilt,
Left the leaves to wither.

Though the palace windows
Had no windowpanes,
Though the doors were doorless
Open to the rains;
Though the marble cupids
Mocked the silent fountain,
People left the house to stand
Empty on the mountain.

Joe, our country neighbor,
Says it isn't so.
Ghosts are in the palace.
Always were, says Joe.
Joe insists there's ashes
Mornings in the grate.
Joe insists an eerie light
Flicks and gutters late.

Seeing branches moving,
Hearing bats and owls,
Joe says every midnight
Someone talks and prowls.
Joe believes as shadows
Brush the gateless gate,
Patrick laughs and loves again
There with Alice Tate.